TICKETS FROM
A BLANK WINDOW

Also by Anne-Marie Fyfe

A House by the Sea
(Bellmead, 1995)

Late Crossing
(Rockingham Press, 1999)

Anne-Marie Fyfe

Tickets from
a Blank
Window

for dear Virginia

with very best wishes

Anne-Marie

24th Nov 2018

Rockingham Press

Published in 2002
by
The Rockingham Press
11 Musley Lane,
Ware, Herts
SG12 7EN

British Library Cataloguing-in-Publication Data

A catalogue record for this book
is available from the British Library

ISBN 1 873468 84 9

Printed in Great Britain
by Biddles Limited
Guildford & King's Lynn

Printed on Recycled Paper

eastengland | arts

in memory of my parents

Alexander Fyfe (1922-1985)
Mary Fyfe, née Reilly (1924-1999)

Acknowledgments

Acknowledgements are due to the editors of the following publications in which some of these poems first appeared: *The Shop, Magma, The Interpreter's House, Poetry Street News, Poetry Wales, The Rialto* and *Smiths Knoll.*

"Wrong Side of the Moon" appeared in *Peterloo Poets: Poetry Competition 1999 Anthology*; "Afternoon on Central Plains Avenue" appeared in *Peterloo Poets: Poetry Competition 2000 Anthology*; "The Elephant Game" and "Art Deco" appeared in *Kent & Sussex Poetry Society: Poetry 2000 Competition Anthology*; "Morning on Bridge Street" appeared in *The Bridport Prize: 2000*; "Winterwood" and "6, Sloop Lane" appeared in *The Tabla Book of New Verse 2001*; "Passing Through Rooms at Eventide" appeared in *Caliban in Prague.*

Contents

I

II

III

IV

I

Though of weak faith, I believe in forces and powers
Who crowd every inch of the air…

Powers, Czeslaw Milosz (tr. with Robert Hass)

LATE CALLER

The woman on the other end
says she's my sister, long lost.

I want to believe but I've lived
too long in the certainty
of no such sibling. Prove it.
Have you slate-blue eyes? Do you
sing? All the women in my family sing.
We have voices like honey.
Do you take night trains? Eat dates?
Fear rivers? And don't suffer fools?
And where the hell were you for the third
decade of the family rosary or
when I wanted a sister to share
late-night dance-hall secrets,
or needed a bridesmaid—
godparent for my firstborn?

Hang up. Press dial-back. My sister
has withheld her number. Didn't say
if she was younger, older, a twin.
It might have made a difference.

WOMEN WHO WAIT

In the dead-headed hour of the storm
she smothers the sleep-stabbing awk of a tern
a wing-pulse away from her glazing, lets surface
that sea-bed of sucked-dry fishbone
and splayed swimmers—too far face-down
for the naked eye—who drift over shipping lines;
as web-fingered masters draw
for first watch, tap thumbnail morses
to their lighthouse brothers who dream
of decks, mizzens, hulks on an ocean
floor. And remember the women who wait.

IN VENICE

You might wake, drenched,
the air around you sinuous
in three-in-the-morning dark;
might even hear the lagoon
lap quattrocento wood piers;
see a woman
bare-shouldered in mist
at the prow of a late *traghetto*.

So you drift back
in the sediments of memory
—schiffling of larch needles,
hail on a skylight,
a rough gear-change on Shore Street—
fall uneasy into fitful sleep
to the insistent slap
of old water on stones.

L'AIR DU TEMPS

It overtakes as he hurries to board
flight 872 from O'Hare
to JFK on a shirt-collar damp
evening, a scent he can't start
to describe. Words like dragonflies flit
in his mind. He registers the backs
of women of the incoming flight,
sure she's here—within reach—
and he has only to find her. He quits
his line and trails walkways and news-stands,
escalators, even the chilled chapel,
catches—like an old tracker dog—
new luggage, old sweat, stale cigar-ends,
on the edge of nausea as each new woman's
scent rattles him further.
It's all he's had of her all these years
and he doesn't begin to know
its name. He finds himself in the duty-free
parfumerie: a crisp, maquillaged
assistant proffers him testers.
Chanel perhaps?... That clear summer—
and now this last chance, but the headiness
of the moment's sensation is slipping.
He tries to hold on like he's holding back
the years in the sharp passages between
nostrils and brain. *Je Reviens?*
she says, *Or Rive Gauche*. From a distance—
then from a more distant distance—
from a much longer way off—
A glass of water, maybe?—her breath
too close to his own, closing in,
at the precise second 872
is lifted clean out of the clouds
and fragments into a dazzling
blue and uncluttered expanse.

MONTANA

On the Montana mountain road return
I pass the Blackspot Roadhouse late;
the only other travelling my way
is tight on my tailgate urging
me into the oncoming glare,
a continuous snaked convoy
of blinded teamsters headed nowhere
I know, some latter-day crossing
facing me down with a battery of near-misses
as the way narrows, markings disappear
and the wavering verge is my one refuge.
Heads insistent in my rearview
send a rancorous message on the revs.

FLEDGING

Little bird—the midwife sighed
handing me a cooing daughter
with a wren-like heartbeat.
Downy wisps trimmed her ears.
Weeks before I noticed
the wings. Tiny harp-shaped scales
nestled in shoulderblades. A gift.

She slept those first winter months
on quilted eider, wakened,
spring days, to birdsong,
twitched infant wings for size.
I heaped mattresses and bolsters
for first flutters from the coalshed,
fed her cod-liver oil and mango,
dried pumpkin-seeds for her lunch-pack.
She grew more sleek with seasons.

Nightly I see her cross landmasses,
oceans, take snow-powdered sierras
in her migratory path, always
on some or other summit, fledging.

VACANT POSSESSION

The spirits of our first real house hung
in years of embossed floral patterns
under layers of flaky wartime distemper.
It wasn't ceiling-damp, the wasp-riddled attic,
the labrador decomposing in a stair-carpet
among shallow lupins. It was rooms that would never
be aired of dying and sniping. The summer
couldn't reach corners. Houseplants yellowed.

Tiffany lamps, a dresser, stripped doors
did little to lift the chill. Our children's
jokes rang in cupboards, hallways, landings.
They complained of a cold underfoot.
Vague histories savaged our night-dreams, days
we woke to a solemn inertia; birdsong
rarely graced our end of the street.
The morning we left, the spirits rumbled,
rattled windows. Razed
the garden shed like a playing-card house,
irked, in the end, at our lack of staying.

THE ELEPHANT GAME

for Ruth

No firm diagnosis: only watch
uneasy as the virus staggers its course,
your lips blueing, blackening. Between
electrodes and scans we play the game
the doctor invented when you said
it began at the fizzy-drink stacks
in Asda that Tuesday afternoon
with elephants cramming the inside of your head,
jumbling, jostling in that fevered space.

So we lead them trunk to tail, toppling
lumbering displays, past frozen mars bars,
coco pops, then coke-can pyramids,
hula-hoops and petits filous
to the extra-wide checkout with their tubs
of double-mint choc-chip. Then crack
the whip, from the top all over again,
while the pain thumps on insistent,
not skipping a beat in your brain.

WINTERWOOD

Through treble-thick stone converted
stable walls I hear a horse canter in puddles
—close-up—bidden slow
at temporary lights on the cobbled way.
Night-bus headlamps sweep drystone
walling. Stark with no passengers
to speak of. A relief driver focuses hard
on the hill-edge poplar windbreak;
awaits the blur of amber; glances
night-skyward, tense with unpredictable hemispheres,
the aligning of planets. And you reach out to me
in the sealed dark of our windowless world,
have me stroke the back of your neck
as I emerge from companies of village ghosts
that follow and find me, far from home
on a street where I've never been,
alighting perhaps from a lit bus that slowed
but never stopped. We slip soundly,
waken to coachouse quiet and the hush of crows.

SIGNALLINGS

Half a land away on a new moon's edge
I hear in the shudder of freefall
that is the verge of sleep, my name
in your accent, the way my father might
have called for a plug-spanner, working blind
in the sudden deeps of a car's engine
back in another country.
           And I'm convinced
in that wayward, instant abyss,
you've homed unannounced, are shouting
from across the landing, skeltering down years
through all the rooms we've lived in,
hanging on for connections on invisible
meridians, through air-corridors, shortwaves,
pounding like a churchbell through time,
velocity, musical static.
           Or do you too
start awake, in a fog-bound ninth-floor
hotel suite in a city that sleeps, start,
to catch my time-delayed signal while we
fumble simultaneously, apart, for light switches,
hunger for that exclamatory surge.

AFTERTASTE

Fallow coming seasons lie unsavoured
by fractured nights. Time to time
I play the game of realising a late
winter infant who won't ever
come home wet to a red door:
won't ever not tie shoelaces or
collect woodlice in a matchbox.
Unguarded circuits dream a half-face,
kindling of a fingernail, mismatch
in a dynasty of nested dolls. And when
haven vanishes in morning hinterlands
I pace the somnolence of high-ceilinged
rooms, nervous floorboards,
relish the undertaste of newness,
quell a quickening leap in my bones.

OUR HOUSE

I come home late to find
my key won't turn in the lock.
Murmurs drift from rooms.
Through the letterbox a child's bike,
a woman's coat on the banister. Beige.
No one answers our door
its scarlet gloss dull now.
I walk up my neighbour's path,
relief as she opens her door.
But she shifts when I say
I'm from next-door. No. Some mistake.
The next-doors are long gone,
no word if they'll ever be back.
People inside? No. Never.
She's not heard a pin drop behind
those walls.
                        When I get back
to our red door they're switching
off lamps, climbing stairs.
Our bedroom is the last to go.

WINTER AFTERNOON

i.m. Michael O'Carroll

In a January stove-stoked schoolroom
with tinsel-wisps and sere holly sprigs
on sills, you slice an onion, illustrate
distillations at the heart of language
while the noonday Aegean ferry docks
hulkingly in spineless wind
and a new intake, ancient hedge-scholars
translated to this second pupillage
disembark into chalk-scented afternoon,
suitcases heavy with winter, packed tight
with fish-hooks, woven name-tapes, *Iliads*.

They bear gifts for a teacher who wears silk ties
and learning lightly – bring crab-apple jelly,
Indian inks, bruised damsons; sit,
a thirsting-for-light half-circle, hush
for your quickening wit, today's thought,
to light, to guard ... to guide
as traceless snails cross your stone-cool floor.

II

> … Outdoors
> The empty bowl of heaven, the empty deep.
> Indoors a purposeful man who talks at cross
> Purposes, to himself, in a broken sleep.
>
> *House on a Cliff*, Louis MacNeice

WRONG SIDE OF THE MOON

Since the night he was never found
his mother wonders what it's like for him
wrong side of the moon, in a rust-riddled
seaplane, the mission easier this time,

no take-off or landing drill, no air-mail
letter home, or tension over cyclones,
electric storms: nothing now
between him and desert stars that move

further as he nears. Must keep alert,
steer clear of the sleep that beckons
in this sky of near-misses. On quiet nights
he hums *South of the Border*, snatches

of *Valencia*, plays the odd game
of gin rummy in his head, filling time
until the dawn that's always on the rise.
He longs for the glow of a just-lit Woodbine,

to skim the forestries of childhood,
hear her whisper, her heart against flight,
Over–my–dead–body
not once, but over and over again.

LANDING

Nighthawks witness his tread on the dead step
seeking her warmth, his body cold as stone
off the night-boat. He'll raise the latch
call her quietly down cobwebs
an octave lower, feel the house's longing
in the heavy hang of the gate,
in the weed-shot paving,
in the front-alcove piano sheeted from years
of missing Sundays.
                    And still in a scrapbook
ordered decades of Telegraph clippings
of the lost-at-sea. Lives printed in water.
Comfort in numbers she'd thought. He catches –
silence;
the fragility of cinders cooling in the grate;
a foghorn off the point;
the lightship's occasional glare.
                    A stone's-throw away
in a hardening plot she misses *the accent
of a coming foot* on the bare landing.

AFTERNOON ON
CENTRAL PLAINS AVENUE

In the suburbs of the lamented it is always late. Rumour
is rife. None has forgotten the rattle of loam on a lid.

Smiles are the order of the day—the week—and neighbours
are hardly at home in the dilapidations of rented rooms.
Phones go unanswered and cat-flaps are sealed.
                                                    Cleaned
uncollected milk-bottles clutter the stoops. Meat safes
are close to high.
                        Singing is rare. Gloves shift
but swimsuits stay on shelves and no-one fears heights.

In the country where snow is general and the undertaker
is king, the only books on loan are elegiac.
Fines are exempted.
                        There is only
one season and just enough light to grow bluebells.

Occasionally someone recalls the headiness
of apple peelings and shutters are locked.
                                    Churchyards
are of the past. Cloud density eclipses the sun
                                            moon and stars.

A SUSPICION OF BUTTERMILK

First he registers the plumbing's going—
relentless drip-drippings that savage the nerves.
Rococo ceiling-work sheds plaster flakes
progressing to deeper faults. Paint would
suffice—if he could choose between matt and silk.
A dead mouse on basement steps atrophies
round its own bone-cage. Northern Line trains
thunder through his cellar like the cow-catcher
on the "3:10 To Yuma" filling the Odeon
screens of his dreams. By day, schoolyard
high-pitch two-streets-off makes him think
of first-borns underwater.

                    Mid-morning.
He lines up library-fines behind Avery
scales. Five months since he's got past the pillar-box.
Airfix precision bombers, perfected
without a tremor, line sills and wooden
draining-boards. A suspicion of buttermilk
clings to Papal-visit tea-towels. Smaller-
than-average flies hover unseasonally
to light on the creaseless beige counterpane.

THE LOVER'S FACE

Gradual – like all mornings – stirred
by the kiss. A divide in the curtains
giving just enough to make him out.
A glint of unease. The lover's
face, true. But a voice somehow tinged.
She waits for familiar inflexions,
tone that will assure, smooth
the day's complexities. She stops
her breath: vowels, syllables, pitch
all wrong, terribly wrong. The edges
of composure begin to slip.
She could revert to sleep, wake again,
from a dream perhaps. She checks—
the line of his nose, the long lobe,
one arched brow, right down to fingernails
where she finds a crescent-shaped
cuticle on a thumb that belongs
to a hand she has never known.
As her eyes scan the face she returns
the slow burn of his petrifying look.

DRY LAND

Three months in the drying the one oil
in years that catches exactly the watery
glaze at the headland will not harden.

Moist as the morning he did it straight off.

Unheard of. He takes to setting canvas
and easel outside in a mid-March breeze.

Soon he's not sleeping; counts each sweep
of lighthouse on plaster-peeled walls.
Takes to muttered beseeching. In wall to wall
night-terrors, chases through the weeping rooms
of the Brera, pressing a discreet thumb
into corners of visitations, calvaries, feels
always the bone-dry stucco he craves.

His headland morning begins to show traces
of the panic—finger-nail indents, smudges.

Hopelessly preserved in all the zest of a day
you could still touch, a watery flawed perfection—
till he notices the rowboat
he'd put in at the slip is halfway along the horizon.

ONE OF THOSE

Eighteen at one count. Every stray in the townland.
But she'd only, she'd say, have four in the kitchen.
The needy. The same fare, though, as the outside cases.
Coddled yolks and a half tin of this month's offer.

The other thing started on the phone somewhere
behind her left ear, she said, a tinny ticking
like a radiator left to cool. *Tinnitus,*
she'd say, when asked, *or one of those.*

Stopped taking the papers. Couldn't fit words to find clues.
Downs dizzier than acrosses. Cats grew sluggish
as the hatchback stagnated on gravel, parcel-shelf
catching the noon nicely low, taking three cats at a stretch.

No one saw her slide the grocery-boxes from the porch.
She unplugged the extension, no longer answered the knocker.

They snaggled over her eiderdown, watched
by a Saint Theresa with broken plaster hands. Even
outsiders, the feral, were slipped in, stealthed round her coma
for days. Then one by one, ravening, moved off into the trees.

LIPREADING THE NEWLY DEAD

No watch or alarm about the place for years
it's the chime not the tick of life he's lost:
a limbo he's lived since her side of the bed
cooled.
    He marks the slippy phases of day
by shadow-length; a parish bell sorts morning
from late, the week from Sunday, its echo
sings long in his blood.
           Novembering he shuffles
the cemetery paths, lipreads the newly dead
on stone. Yellow school-register names.
                 In mirrors
he catches himself thorn-crowned, in a belted
gaberdine, as they bay him with pebbles on Main Street
on a downpour day of a sheepsale.
               As light flits
bands of children rattle latches, spit miscallings
down his hall, chant louder as they reel.

Mornings, shriven, he wakes to the eggshell shiver
of an angel's wing: prostrates on cool
linoleum before a God he's never loved.

Her letter will be here any day. He'll pack
a light shirt, the ounce of ready-rubbed put by,
a battery torch just in case. He'll set out in overgrowth
head high without a care for it will be
morning, the stillest time, and high season.

INHERITANCE

He walks at night with the father
he never knew in a shroud-brown shirt
to the news-stand on the corner. He counts
mother-of-pearl studs, two for each
cuff. Wakes in a cold sweat. He can never
catch the face at an angle he remembers.
In stains of mildewed mirrors
he glimpses the grown-up dead,
scans for genetic imprints, examines
irregular whorls on finger-tips, visualises
his father's preserved on a comb
fallen, maybe, down the back of a sideboard.
Running his tongue on his teeth's
upper edge, he wonders if his father's felt the same.

WHITE-OUT

She wakes to a chiller chill, a fine
off-white dust coating every surface:
one snow-capped shoe on the fireplace rug,
frost-patterns on a wardrobe mirror,
a stiffening veil on the skirt she draped
on the french-weave chair last night.

She imagines in the glen a school bus
jack-knifed in swathes of it, the driver
clearing spadefuls, whistling ice
through the gap in his teeth.
                              A sigh puffs
as near-cold ash collapses in the grate.

She hears the car start-up in the lane,
skid some, spin for a small lifetime—
flail in first—second—then—
relax in third. The arctic canopy
covering her knees begins to thaw
turns to glacial water that must
seep blotting-paper-quick to her heart.

NEXT SUMMER

He paces every circumference inch
in his head. All weathers. Twice-yearly leaves the house
in search of rucksacks, film, zippered macs.
Has walking shoes re-heeled at intervals.

Thoughts of air-travel trouble his heart.

He plots itineraries, treks, Greyhound routes
with a stubbing forefinger at breakfast. Cities are
his *metier*. He can locate spires, bridges, waterways
of Venice, the intersections of Montreal. He sings
phrase-books by rote, checks daily fluctuations
in dinars, zlotys, thumbs the small print in Baedeker.

He numbers maps for reference, worries that
worn folds could obliterate a *piazza*, *rue*, *námestí*,
frets he might one day become a stranger adrift.

The compass by his bedside rocks gently on North.
When he surfaces in the early hours to fight the dark,
he pictures cut-outs of Pacific night beyond ceiling, roof,
hears lashing that can only be Monsoon.

DAMP IN HER BONES

At the interment she doesn't protest—
long days hold few surprises
and the same quiet for all.
She tells Scheherazade-stories
but ones with a scorpion's sting.
The familiar grinds to a snail
—she has all the time in the world—
takes slow trains to Iowa, bakes
boysenberry pie on low heat,
plays the opening bars of scales.
Soon she learns to spot the genesis
of weeds, subterranean saplings,
can feel damp in her bones months ahead.
The bell-towers and schoolrooms of home
seem to be losing focus.

She doesn't miss night or the confusions of waking,
misses: the red of tulips; tea in bone china;
a man's breath. Fear of death soon goes—
but fear does not.
                    Sometimes a mockingbird
loops and circles her patch. Often it's buzzards.
She waits for the long snowings-in of winter.

PASSING THROUGH ROOMS
AT EVENTIDE

They resume each night in the balm of aniseed—
wedding-album poses under disconnected
room-lights, make small-talk in Amish
shirt-collars, play Persian Roulette with blanks,
turnabout, blindfold for that 100% frisson
as the wireless submerges between wave-lengths.
He thumbs a nightly gazetteer that once was
her uncle's; she pats another day's undone
needlepoint, ochre-yellow skeins oily
from overfingering. Step-for-step they prowl
the apartment's temperate regions
checking for drippy faucets; he plays,
in passing, arpeggios on a hall-cold upright.
Relentless, she readies clocks, rewinds,
sets each to a different time-frame
and sashays like a girl who waits to be kissed.
A girl who wants to be kissed. Properly.

III

Tonight I saw myself in the dark window as
the image of my father ...

Mirror Image, Louise Glück

MARRIAGE LINES

In the dogday of a foundling summer
I sift baptismal ledgers, standing
in need of a turning point, a trail
to the tall untalked-about grandfather
whose mid-afternoon grew dark
with the slow losing of the girl
in eyeletted boots. Their elopement had coincided
with the Rising: irreparable sunderings.

The Virginia road is borderline,
a montbretia-blazed funeral crawl behind balers
in a gustless sky-cleansing downpour.
Nothing between copperplate lines;
the churchyards keep none of his brothers.
A country of roadside blackspot-grottoes,
early-closings and rock-hard sweets in clouded jars.
Roadsides that have the cure
for everything but the heart.

MY OTHER

The mer-child me is flame-headed,
frecklish, silver-quick—saves
dried sea-horses in sardine-tins,
trades teeth for cones with chocolate
vermicelli. The mer-girl ducks
summer spray watching for
rainbows that fail to reach
the light-rock, her squid-ink sketches
have no sign of parents. An imaginary
friend has lurex scales, knows
motorbikes, ferris-wheels—surfaces
near Limerick Point after ten,
clandestine. The mer-girl-me
tells purposeful lies. Her known world
deepens overnight. She traces
crustacean fossils, collects
sea-artichokes and pink-black pearls
by a quarter moon. Her favourite
pillow is a bloated Penguin
Moby Dick, long, long overboard. She
knows she can outlive turtles, myths.

WIDOW

From our scooped-out treehouse in a high box-hedge
—den of dented saucepans, kettleless lids
and two years of curling Look-and-Learns—
we'd monitor our rarely-sighted neighbour.

Forty years after his death took her
from hill station to our bleak promontory
she kept to her shrine of rattan chaises,
translucent tea-sets and elephant gods,
wore turbanned hats, layered silks for everyday.

Half her home, nestling in pines, was a painted
railway carriage that once crossed borders,
hauled ordnance and freight over creepered ravines
to a north-west frontier.
                              Times we'd see her progress
halt on mosaic steps, catch her stooped
on an late verandah as summer moths
flickered darkly round kerosene mantles.

HALLOWEVE

On the red candlewick edge,
a lit Price's candle in one hand,
apple from Hannah's in the left,
I'm waiting for my promised's face
in the photo-booth blackness
of my grandmother's cheval.
No hazelnut irises manifest
above my right shoulder, no sound
beyond Angela's keyhole breath and the tick
of a wedding-present eight-day clock;
as-yet unspoken-for names jostle
at gables as the heart hammers.
At that moment he might be
splitting a monkey-nut shell—
rubbing a vaccination mark
under his sleeveless fair-isle
as my teeth puncture apple-skin.

THE BIG PICTURE

A fly-paper yellowy Sunday and she's up there
panning for proofs: bare parish-register
facts; exam practice-papers in a Clarks'
shoe-box; Kodak snaps
with communion shoe-straps; fixed
running-board children's smiles, last seen
in disregarded handbags on the low shelf
of a tallboy; a vanity case with folded
Canadian bills in ruched pockets.
Faces torn from photos
by hopeful former boyfriends
no longer count. Familiar borrowings
read now like her own—the tale of a brother
taking an unhomeward blizzard turning
after the Christmas Day matinee—
It's a Wonderful Life—scenes flickering
off the screen's edge for a shuddering hour.

ANTITHESES

There is innocence in wooden buttons,
spiralbounds, winter journeys.
There is knowing in the transferred epithet,
swing-doors, dog-dream yelps.
Innocence in a spring tide,
snow peas, a stopped red bus.
Knowledge in undealt hands,
remote controls, a Chekhov sky.
Innocence is an after-kiss,
mochaccino froth, an inner-city pocket-map.
There is knowingness in dial-back,
two-way mirrors, the crematorium smoke-stack.

INVENTORY

Tide-warped ajar oak-effect front door.
HALLWAY: left.
RECEPTION: posed family group, marquetry frame.
CELLAR: scuttle; curling wallpaper rolls; snail-silvered
brickwork; a summer's must in unstoppered jars.
BACK BEDROOM: tallboy; orange-blossom... maybe;
moth-balls in going-away-suit pockets; padded
damson satin clothes-hanger; shoe-box of Mass cards.
DOLLSHOUSE ATTIC: broken hasp; toneless
whisper of a child's rockabye; knitting-machine,
no value.
BATHROOM: moulding cheval-glass; Gillettes
rust-stuck to shelf-paint; kirbygrips, Euthymol,
Germolene; plastic fish curtains.
SCULLERY: Pyrex dinner-set; draining-board;
tea-stained sink-tidy.
LARDER: blue-rim basin; cutlery dividers;
soup-barley in Horlicks jars lumpen;
absent crackle of October toffee-apple baking trays.

REEL FOUR

When the projectionist opens the last can
I'll be watching for that hand-held sequence
from our black-and-white days
where we eat our first *pizza á l'oeuf*
off the map in a Marais courtyard,
crumbly-stuccoed, gas-lit,
in a nightsphere groggy with *estragon*
and the headswims of *Nuit Étoilée*—
and after, pulses easing like a city slows,
smoothing raincoats beneath municipal shrubs
we sleep, weary from the toll
of a rucksack great with tomorrows.

SLIPPAGES

Unsettled arguments shunt behind clocks,
in ceiling cracks, as apples cosied
in deaths-pages tremble softly in the attic.
The house jolts for her in odd instants:
the finding of her father's cuff-link in an unlined
drawer, oxidated as a last breath.

She rewalks May processions, dead-headed
petals, relives this morning's mourning
vision, night condensing always
opaque on glass. Easterlies probe
uneven dark while she hunts clues,
a head's pillow-centre impression, lone
feathers alighting on the undusted ledge.

Open wounds sting with desire for
September blaeberrying, honeyed pulp
dried in creases of a wicker basket.

Days that were days, and were ours,
till incremental subsidence set in
with the postman's departing tread,
softly, and desertion came into its own.

6, SLOOP LANE

In a night air thick with low tide
and shadows of long-ago children
I trace that holiday-let among blind
alleys stepped up from the harbour.

I want you to know that the house
is smaller than I remember
an ill-fitted screen door and withered
Chronicles, a flat tube of glue
among flies on a teak windowshelf.

Promenade hotels echo too few residents.

But you'd still know the out-of-hours dentist's
close by on the hill where I fretted with an abscess,
the gents' outfitters where we found
the stormcoat that never quite fitted.

I want to tell you every last
tang-laden, mast-clinking bit of it
but even if I could mail you
or waken the dead call-collect
you'd want to know what
in this world I was talking about.

TICKETS FROM A BLANK WINDOW

Last night at last I caught the train
to Summertown, eight thirty-five,
I took a ticket from a blank window.
The tannoy coughed a small delay.
And then. A route I feel I know.
The city draws away from me:
I stare into the backs of lives
still living out in lighted rooms where
stories flick and go.
               No sleeping car,
I settle in my winter coat and
watch the window-woman's face. What
changes will you see when I step down?

So many times I've thought about
your waiting there, mornings when the guard
would catch the mail and raise his flag
and you would walk away.

IV

The mother ties the hair-ribbons of the child
and she has peace.

Extraordinary References, Wallace Stevens

LATE IN THE EVENING

She doesn't say much in the weeks after
admission: voices from before
disfigure vacuous evenings
as visitors reverse darkwards
catching by the main gates a fox's
listless fear. Abandoned she observes
how she side-steps to Geraldo full-on,
on a hairsbreadth station, submerging
random echoes of missed loves, scratching
images of undreamt babies; turns
her head towards her only child's muffles
from miles off
                    or from a star-lit sycamore
brushing the night-secure fire-escape
by her room at the eaves of the world

RAUCOUS SILENCES

Needle-stuck birdsongs contend
with failing of brakes. At one
remove. A slammed door. My mother's
glazed rabbit—one of a wedding pair—
mocks with its cocked broken ear
from the window's tiled shelf.
I skew, flinch from that bluish
mordant eye. Looking-glass vertigo
steadies as wilted gold stamp-hinges
curl in the leavings of sunset.
Clamorous night-cream contaminates
in lidless black jars. Lost lists spill
from drawers, clichéd bitter intentions.
At the same remove, a weightless voice
resurrects itself breathless
in the anaesthesia of a keyhole.

WOOL SHOPS

She comes to in the pallid absence
of infant warmth soured on her tongue.
Middle fingers blister-red
from endless purling of unfinished
matinee coats, frantic counting of stripes,
vigilant waiting for dropped
stitches, unravelling of selvedges.

Strains for that first hint
through the wall. Step by step:
bath, layette, milk
to just below boiling, mash rusk,
the rehearsed rubrics. And then wool shops.
More solid colours. Reverse sequence in yellow.
Fine lines of carmine for definition.
She moves her head towards a call
that is just too far for ease.
Maybe a touch of green
to break things up, complete
the pattern before casting off.

FIRST HOUSES

On bright Cold-War afternoons
before I started Mill Street School
my mother taught me the perfect lip
and curve of a cup and saucer—
then a solid, angled house
with endwalls and sloping gable:
I'd add the tied-back curtains,
front door with a seven,
borders of big-leaf flowers
crayoned neatly to the line.

When I wanted to know if her mother
had taught her to do house-numbers
she told me about the illness,
about going away to her grandfather's,
not seeing her mother again.

I soon forgot to include the curl
of chimney-smoke, my eaves
went wobbly, shutters less straight,
the seven barely readable.
I stopped drawing perfect homes.
For nice families.
Even before my mother got sick.

EXPECTED/LANDED

Double-tucking non-fitted corners
I hold as late flights spiral
in the city's evening uprush,
glance momentarily clockward
closing the guest-room door;
then over Arrivals espresso
bid myself not notice how
thin or pale you've become,
not fuss when you drift
in the third row of *Oklahoma*
or over sole still on-the-bone.
And I surely won't question why
you're here on an open ticket
with a suitcase lighter than feathers.

SHORT LET

In the orphaned aeons of sleep
I repack the latest in a long life
of muffled suitcases, fret
that I can't place one child's
fair-isle mittens, the ones
with the untangled cord. An edge
to make skin creep as bleached
daylight threads the gap
in back-room curtains.
Scenes from obsequies in waxy
parish light. I juggle
this morning's buff envelopes
with the mounting gaggle of keys
sure the clutch will renege
at the first sign
of pressure on Scott's Hill.

FIRST GRAVEDIGGER

A kaleidoscope of stairwells, alcoves, slanting
linoleum patterns recedes on waking;
leaves me unsteady on the shores of today.
Heartfelt ticks of strange clocks
nag as a flickering neon "VACANCIES"
dances unseasonably outside my window.
Each day the boatman skirts
the first headland for seven-and-six.
I see him toothless on rusted rungs
counting florins with fingerpads hard
from a lifetime's wrestling the under-tow,
Saturdays spent clearing dry
bones from new graves. Draughts whinny
around my door-frame, catch nape-hairs.
I exhale slowly; turn from the light.

TIDAL REACHES

Shoals of the predestined
lie side-curled in small coracles.
Nameless, they backstroke
into being on the turn of a current,
cloaks masking misshapen form,
eyes opaque and unforgiven.
Shamelessly they court the living
beyond ankle-deep, calf-high,
abandoning them with a sideways look
that would say—*shores lie just beyond*
that headland shifting in mist.
Laughter punctuates their low cacophony.

ROCKPORT

Sou'westered on rocks below
my salted window, he might be
a trawlerman back from deep-sea.
Look again and I make out only
white stones, stepped in the dark.
The daddy-long-legses that death-danced
these rooms lately have today
surrendered on carpets and curtains,
drowned in plugholes, and the creakings
of this holiday-let jar. They are not the surings
of home where a slamming red door
below is followed by your sprint
on the stair. An ill-wind troubles
flaking eaves and talk in the town
of trees down and promised power-cuts unsettles.
The boy next door has ten-and-a-half sunflowers
in his front yard. He says I should take
polaroids of them. Nothing
to do but be there for the mail-van
rounding the promontory to fill my days.

UNIFORMS OF SNOW

Full heads pick up gravestones, railings,
as I leave town for another
bedside night of her troubled
breathing—and think of him in there
long-buried and waiting.

He'll have known for weeks now,
have sensed the willing hesitancy,
known she'll make it in the end,
sons and grandsons carrying her
the last measured journey.

I flick small hurried rainspots
from the windscreen, pursue
a snaking recent skid-line
for half a mile or more, alive
to the nearness of ditches and death.

That frost-packed length of earth
—unbroken half of the double-plot—
will take some shifting: he'd be keen
to see her settled before snow,
before December tightens its grip.

ART DECO

Unable to rise now for two weeks and a day
she says she only wants a mirror to check
how that last wash-and-set is holding.

I invent excuses. An unnamed queasiness.

Late on, at her washbasin mirror
as I empty the evening's unsipped-at 7-Up,
I catch that days-off-death look
again and watch how
                              thinking herself unseen
she reaches in her handbag.

With slow fingers she prises the fluted
compact lid, the one I'd brought all the way
from Macy's one Christmas, the powder
even on winter days a touch too pale
for her liking: she looks long enough to see
all she needs to know, snaps the compact,
releases the invisible sweetness of dust.

COURTYARD

The ring-road hospital bird-table boasted
starlings, pigeons—swaggerers
she had no time for. She was glad
when the treatment ended.
                              Then
at the nursing home a man with a ladder
and nail hung a nylon bag
of peanuts at her window.

For weeks she watched small birds nibble,
kept an eye on when I'd last eaten.
As curtains closed early and she slept longer
I'd wonder if their flittering struggled
through her sleep. And I'd breathe
again each daybreak to tiny wingbeats
and her picking at crumbs of toast.

Clearing her room on the third of December
I stretch to wrestle the empty string bag,
lose it to a sudden bitter wind.

MORNING ON BRIDGE STREET

This new address is lighter than airmail:
on blue my street-name looks faint, watered.
I unwrap my mother's fine-bone chattels,
sugar-bowl crazy with hairline fissures.
In 5 a.m. still, the locals aver
that time hangs slow, conscious of being
a stone's throw from the not-long dead
who thrive on such broken mornings. The blind
accordion-player on the bridge hollers
it's the real, the absolute, time of day.
Thanks you for the chink of currency.
Passers-by strain to catch his underplayed
wheeze. The postman abandons his route
in small hours. Residents
listen out for a noiseless whistle.

UNMARKED ROAD

Her settling grave is not on any plan:
evenings in and out of weather
you try but the post at the crossroads
—its leeward list sharpened over years—
is less and less precise,
half a mile, it says, or three
and seven-eighths—you set out
footwise, unsure to noplace
you could know. Leave however early
you'll not outwit the wind that thwarts
your making the gates by light. Know that
the arrow switches, swings behind your back.
Catch in an eye's corner
the backdraught of a wingbeat
you know from old films. It skits
nightward and you can't help
checking your throat for marks—
until yielding you find yourself
backing off from that once when
you'll arrive there, timely, early,
see the sign unswivelled.

CHARTREUSE

The woman at the corner of Sunset
and Main in the dilute green of evening
is wearing my mother's face.

                I shadow,
in determined steps, feet that make no
mark on rain-wet paving—follow
but can't close, stalling over gaps
between slabs from habits of caution,
dragging my hold-all of unrhyming
cadences and broken glassware.

                    She pauses
at a black-edged postcard in the hardware
window, quizzes diffident strangers
about a lost rosary, the whereabouts
of motherless infants, shifts through
ill-lit laneways as shop-fronts dissolve,
whole streetfuls of them.

                I search
the night-long map for a woman
wearing my mother's face. Her face.